INTRODUCTION

RE-DISCOVERING THE PAST

Why new editions of Discovering the Past?

SHP's Discovering the Past series has become one of the most widely used Key Stage 3 resources around the country. The core texts *Contrasts and Connections*, *Societies in Change* and *Peace and War* are in use in almost half of all secondary schools. The Special Needs Support Materials by Colin Shephard, Ann Moore and Barbara Brown have extended the use of this material into nearly all contexts, from those students with extreme learning difficulties to the most able candidates. The key features which made those original materials so widely adopted were that they successfully provided:

- a coherent course
- an issue-based approach
- real classroom appeal
- careful planning for differentiation
- plentiful source-based investigations
- constant opportunities for in-depth work
- meaningful tasks involving real enquiry and communication which allow pupils to construct their own view of the past.

These key features have not dated. They are still the bedrock of effective practice. And the books are still very widely used and will continue to be. These are the qualities that led *Teaching History* to describe the Discovering the Past series as 'history teaching at its best' – a rare accolade for a textbook. *Discovering Medieval Realms* was awarded the *TES* Secondary Schoolbook Award in 1993.

This new foundation level mini-series does not replace those books. Rather, it updates the core units to provide an alternative streamlined diet, particularly for schools which found the original series inaccessible for some pupils.

At the same time

- the review of the National Curriculum,
- the new understanding of the role of literacy and thinking skills in the teaching of history,

- the appearance of schemes of work for Key Stage 3, and
- the increasing emphasis on scaffolding pupils' extended writing and their conceptual development

have all allowed the editors of this edition to take a second look at the original and recast it in the light of these developments.

This new series has attempted to take the core material from the Britain 1750–1900 unit of *Peace and War*, prune it, and remix it to provide a truly accessible textbook for mixed-ability teaching, yet one which is still based on the principles of in-depth investigation and varied styles of enquiry that drove the first editions.

Key features of the new Pupils' Book

- **Redesign:** these new editions have been totally redesigned. A simple visual style has been adopted throughout, avoiding clutter.
- **The author's text** has been made as simple and accessible as the content allows. There is less text and what text there is makes more use of story.
- **Extended writing:** there were many opportunities for analytical and discursive extended writing in the first edition. These opportunities have been accentuated, and support for these tasks, in the form of writing frames, tables and grids, has been provided in the Pupils' Book and in this Teachers' Resource Book (later referred to as TRB). A new addition is the Story Writing activity which begins on page 23. A story recipe and a story-planning table support this, as does Worksheet 9.
- **Differentiation:** all tasks can be further differentiated. Opportunities for differentiation exist within the Pupils' Book; by using this TRB; or by using the Special Needs Support Materials.
- **National Curriculum review:** all content is totally in line with the emphasis of the revised National Curriculum, both the statutory elements and the learning approaches suggested by the schemes of work.

- **In-depth work:** the material offers plentiful opportunities for in-depth study, whilst also providing the option of an overview of each topic studied.
- **Structure:** all enquiries have been clearly structured so that pupils can easily find the material they need to answer a question; so that the relationship of each spread to an overall task is always clear; and so that non-specialist teachers may find it easier to use this material.
- **Space:** one third of the material in the first edition has been deleted entirely. We hope we have not deleted your favourite bit! However, we can't get it right for every user. In deciding what to keep we have been guided by user feedback. So what remains is much more spaced out. What is really needed can now work effectively because it has the space to do so.
- **Special needs support:** throughout we have tried to ensure that we have built on and developed the teaching ideas from Colin Shephard and Barbara Brown's Special Needs Support Materials (SNSM) which have been so effective in the teaching of history to lower attainers. These new books will fit in with the SNSM very well. There is a summary of the links on page 7 of this TRB.
- **Challenge:** this new series aims to be totally accessible to average ability pupils while not losing SHP's characteristic emphasis on challenging pupils and teachers alike.

- **Variety:** the material aims to remain flexible and varied. You will find some short enquiries; some long ones; some games; some feature spreads; some creative writing; some analytical writing. We have tried to avoid a rigid or formulaic approach.
- **Story:** throughout the series we have made greater use of narrative and story to set the context for source-based work and to develop historical understanding.
- **Source-based work:** there are fewer written sources and more visual ones. The series continues SHP's characteristic use of source-based work, but this work, like all else in the new editions, will be carefully structured and targeted on the investigations where source-based work is helpful and engaging to the pupil.
- **New material:** there are totally new enquiries in each unit. In this unit the material on Britain and India (pages 54–59) is new. Most enquiries have at least one new spread. Some enquiries have been grouped into more coherent longer enquiries such as those within Depth Study 2: Empire and trade. All have new ideas for teaching and learning.

The Teachers' Resource Book

The entire effort of the revision of the Pupils' Book has been towards accessibility. The worksheets in this TRB are designed with the same principle in mind. They offer still greater accessibility to the core tasks of the Pupils' Book.

RE-DISCOVERING BRITAIN 1750–1900

Aims

What is history about? QCA has spelled out its vision with the revised National Curriculum. Many of its points echo those which formed the rationale of the original Schools History Project and which have driven SHP's curriculum development ever since.

History aims to:

- stimulate pupils' curiosity
- help pupils to engage with the past
- develop pupils' sense of identity (individually and collectively)
- help pupils to appreciate diversity and to value inheritance
- help clarify pupils' life choices
- allow pupils to see how the past influences the present
- develop distinctive, disciplined, problem-solving methods, critical enquiry skills, thinking skills and communication skills, all of which will be immensely useful in the quickly changing world of the 21st century.

These are big aims. History is a big subject. These are the aims of *Re-Discovering Britain 1750–1900*.

Content

Content was always an issue in National Curriculum History. In fact most of the debate about the early versions of it was almost entirely about content – what was in, what was out! And at school level, the problem of coverage – 'How do I fit it all in?' – has often dominated curriculum planning.

In theory at least the new National Curriculum removes this problem. None of the content of the old Expansion, Trade and Industry unit is now compulsory in the newly named 'Britain 1750–1900' unit. Only the focus of the unit is now prescribed. You could therefore decide to tackle Key Stage 3 in a radically new way (and SHP can help you here too, since alongside this series SHP has developed This is History!, a new series of books which provide a radical **new scheme of work** for all who relish the opportunity to innovate).

In *Re-Discovering Britain 1750–1900* our approach has been different. We have stayed with what has become the canon of the 'Britain 1750–1900' unit, but have used the flexibility of the new curriculum to let us focus our attention on the parts of the unit which have acquired an accessibility track record over the past decade. So in this book there are no content surprises.

Overview

The major activity in the overview of the period is for pupils to describe and then explain the changes between 1750, 1825 and 1900.

Depth Study 1 explores the impact of the Industrial Revolution on people's lives. The major activities look at the causes of this revolution through the lives of two men, Wedgwood and Arkwright, and its impact upon workers through the example of children in cotton mills. The review activity invites pupils to reach a judgement on the question: How did the Industrial Revolution change things?

Depth Study 2 covers the wide area of the British Empire and trade within it. The aim is for pupils to examine aspects of this area, essentially through case studies of the West Indies and India, in order to consider who benefited and, conversely, who did not.

Depth Study 3 is another substantial enquiry looking at towns. It has as its central thread an examination of the stereotype that Victorian towns were foul places. It achieves this by looking at Liverpool, Manchester, Brighton and London.

Depth Study 4 looks at political changes. The focus is on two points: the demand for reform culminating in the 1832 Reform Act and Chartism. The review activity asks pupils to evaluate to what extent things changed.

Depth Study 5 explores the ideas of the Victorians. It does this through a number of individuals, real and fictional. The pupils gradually build up a picture of what the Victorians believed so that they can reach their own opinion of that value system.

The overview is essential to pupil understanding but the depth studies can be put together in a variety of ways. The National Curriculum describes this unit as 'a study of how expansion of trade and colonisation, industrialisation and political changes affected the United Kingdom, including the local area'. This requirement can be met by using all five depth studies. You might choose to omit parts of an enquiry, such as looking just at India in Depth Study 2, without detracting from the overarching enquiry task. It is also possible to omit Depth Studies 3 and 5 and still meet National Curriculum requirements. Your decision will most likely be determined by the potential for local history in your area.

Skills, knowledge and understanding

The term 'key elements' has disappeared from the revised National Curriculum, although all the ideas remain under the 'Skills, knowledge and understanding' heading (see page 4). These same ideas suffuse the attainment target. This unit gives plentiful opportunities to develop work on all these elements. The detailed teachers' notes point to the most important opportunities for each.

Skills, knowledge and understanding	Example
Chronological understanding **1** To develop their chronological understanding pupils should be taught to: **a)** recognise and make appropriate use of dates, vocabulary and conventions that describe historical periods and the passing of time.	Timeline (pages vi–1)
Knowledge and understanding **2** To develop their knowledge and understanding pupils should be taught to:	
a) describe and explain the relationships between the characteristic features of specified periods and societies including the experiences and range of ideas, beliefs and attitudes of people in the past;	What made Richard Arkwright successful? (pages 16–21)
b) consider the social, cultural, religious and ethnic diversity of the societies studied, both in Britain and the wider world;	The different faces of London (pages 78–83)
c) describe, analyse and explain reasons for, and results of, the historical events, situations and changes in the periods studied;	Activity: Why was slavery abolished? (pages 50–53)
d) identify trends, both within and across periods, by making links between the content in different areas of study and between local, British (or United Kingdom as appropriate), European and world history;	Britain and India: joined by a thread (pages 54–59).
e) consider the significance of the main events, people and changes studied.	Review: How did the Industrial Revolution change things? (page 32)
Historical interpretation **3** To develop their understanding of how history is represented and interpreted pupils should be taught:	
a) how and why some historical events, people, situations and changes have been interpreted differently;	Review: Was there more to a Victorian town than 'foul facts'? (page 84)
b) to evaluate interpretations.	Children in the mills (pages 22–29)
Historical enquiry **4** To develop their skills of historical enquiry pupils should be taught to: **a)** carry out enquiries into aspects of the areas of study from a range of appropriate sources of information including oral accounts, documents, printed sources, the media, artefacts, pictures, photographs, music and using the resources of museums, buildings and sites, and ICT;	Britain's slave trade: the inside story (pages 38–49)
b) identify appropriate sources for carrying out an enquiry into an aspect of the past, evaluate the sources in their historical context, collect and record information relevant to the enquiry and reach conclusions.	What did the Victorians believe? (pages 100–105)
Organising and communicating **5** To develop their skills of organising and communicating pupils should be taught to: **a)** recall, prioritise and select historical information;	Review: How did the Industrial Revolution change things? (page 32)
b) organise historical information by the accurate selection and use of chronological conventions and historical vocabulary appropriate to the periods studied;	Review: Did anything really change? (page 98)
c) communicate their knowledge and understanding of history, using a range of techniques, including spoken language, structured narratives, substantiated explanations and making use of ICT.	Children in the mills – Story Writing activity (page 23)

Using this material in the classroom

Enquiries
Each unit is split into a number of enquiries. The enquiry is a discrete piece of work on a discrete theme with a major written or tangible outcome. Each enquiry covers a number of pages in the Pupils' Book.

An enquiry has a heading like this:

Why was British industry so successful?

Each of the depth study opening pages has a strong visual image. This is intended to provoke discussion and give you the opportunity to hook pupils' interest. The scope and purpose of the depth study are also outlined on the opening pages. Make sure pupils know the aims of any piece of work they are about to undertake.

Choices
We are assuming that most schools will want to give approximately a term's teaching time to this book. An enquiry might take up to three weeks, with or without homework. However, given that schools spend such varying amounts of time on history – at the last QCA/OFSTED count six per cent was a Y9 average but time allocation was falling – we have had to build in a great deal of flexibility, and choices will have to be made by you, the teacher, about what to focus on, and what to omit.

Preparation
Before starting out on an enquiry always read the activities in the Pupils' Book and the detailed notes in this TRB.

The book has been written with the expectation that much of the material will be introduced by the teacher in whole-class teaching. It might be that you read a spread through with the class, or it might be that you simply use the information it provides to set the scene for pupils in your own way, before they proceed to the activity.

The degree of teacher input is the main agent of differentiation. One key belief in all of the books in this series is that all pupils should attempt similar activities. Therefore flexible support material is provided here so that you are able to vary the level of support pupils receive, or the challenge they face.

Major tasks
At the end of most enquiries there is a major piece of work bringing together the work covered. The main purpose of the rest of the activities in each enquiry is to provide access to this major task for all pupils.

However, we are not rigid about this. Part of the appeal of the SHP material is due to the easily usable **feature spreads**, which demand to be used in their own right. Not every piece of history has to have a rigorous written outcome. The mistaken assumption that it does is one of the unfortunate side effects of the current focus on extended writing. At times the historical objective will be to have some fun, therefore encouraging the pupils to engage with the past sufficiently to allow learning to develop. Stimulating curiosity and engaging pupils with the past is vitally important and in terms of preparation for adult life stands head and shoulders above teaching an erudite yet obscure aspect of historical content. So we don't look down on good fun – we just try to make sure it takes you somewhere!

Assessment
These major tasks are also the main opportunity for assessing pupils' progress and compiling evidence of attainment. In addition, there are review activities at the end of each depth study which bring together pupils' work on a wide range of topics and which form significant assessment opportunities.

Group work and encouragement
Many of the activities assume group work. In this book pupils are working with new ideas, skills and problems for much of the time. If pupils are worried about 'getting it wrong' they will play safe and their progress will be hindered. Group work can help here. Some pupils experiment more in small groups because they are not so worried about getting things wrong. But even more important is teacher reaction and encouragement. Any genuine attempts to tackle the questions should be encouraged.

Process questions
In order to free up space for the major tasks and to avoid clutter on the page we have taken the en route 'process questions' out of the Pupils' Book entirely – that is, those that appeared in yellow boxes in the earlier edition of this unit.

Sources
Consistent with our aim of accessibility, we have translated, simplified and edited written source material where necessary. Spelling and punctuation have been made contemporary. Modern equivalent words have often been substituted where necessary, or definitions provided. However, the sense and meaning of all sources have been preserved.

It is sound practice to read and discuss all the sources with pupils. We are attempting to develop pupils' skills and understanding, which will not be achieved by simply leaving them to get on by themselves all the time.

Source lines

The source line – which introduces and describes the source being studied – is an important tool for the pupil. It contains the details pupils need to know to answer any questions, such as who wrote or painted the source, and when. Encourage pupils to see these source lines as an important part of the evidence.

Detailed teachers' notes

There are detailed teachers' notes for each enquiry starting on page 8 of this book. These detailed notes provide:

- help on how to introduce a topic
- suggestions on which questions to use for discussion and which for written work
- ideas for support or extension work – including links to photocopiable worksheets in this TRB and in the associated SNSM
- suggested resources.

Worksheets

For each unit there are also a number of photocopiable worksheets. These provide extension and support material. Some are designed to be suitable for homework where it is impracticable for pupils to use the Pupils' Book itself.

Timelines

The unit covers a period of 150 years. When you begin the unit it is a good idea, where feasible, to cover the whole of one wall of the classroom with a timeline. As progress is made through the unit, pupils' work can be displayed at appropriate points on the timeline. Don't put too many dates on this main timeline (more dates can go on the pupils' own version of the timeline); concentrate instead on the relationships between the elements.

Differentiation

This book forms part of a flexible package. In addition to this book there is:

- a mainstream unit (Britain 1750–1900 in *Peace and War*)

- a 240-page Teachers' Resource Book containing worksheets for special needs support

- a Picture Pack which covers the unit through visual source material alone

- a Workbook to support the Picture Pack.

Opportunities therefore abound for differentiation by task, by input or by degree of support. Full details of these other resources are on the back cover of this book.

The detailed notes highlight the support offered by the SNSM. The matrix overleaf summarises these links.

Enquiry	SNSM tasks
Overview	1
How did Britain change between 1750 and 1900?	2–4
What made Richard Arkwright successful?	5, 6
Children in the mills	22–24
What was the British Empire for?	40, 41
Britain's slave trade: the inside story	29, 30, 39
Why was slavery abolished?	31
Foul facts!	3, 4
Why did Liverpool and Manchester need a railway?	17–19
The different faces of London	11, 42
Was there more to a Victorian town than 'foul facts'?	10
What was wrong with democracy in the 1820s?	37
Were the Chartists revolutionaries?	38
How did the Victorians try to help the poor?	33–36
Why did Annie Besant want to help poor people?	28

Cross-curricular issues

ICT

Communication is clearly a core skill of history. ICT applications such as word-processing programs, DTP programs, graphics programs, scanning software and presentational software can all be used effectively to work on the major tasks in this book.

It is an essential part of the historical thought process to move ideas around, to try grouping ideas in different ways, to refine tentative conclusions in the light of new evidence, and to introduce new findings or further corroborating evidence into a written answer. Word-processing packages make this more feasible than ever before.

Other ICT applications can really enhance historical learning, such as databases to handle data, and graphics and design programs to help with presentation. In this way ICT can form an essential part of creating a good piece of historical writing.

Internet research is now a staple when studying or teaching history. The number of suitable and well-maintained sites is increasing so rapidly it is impossible to write an up-to-date listing!

The problem, however, is always what pupils do with the information once they get to a site! Too much information, too little analysis, is the bane of internet research. So, whatever research you set up, ensure that the historical enquiry remains at the forefront of pupils' minds. For example, do not just ask pupils to find out about a person such as Josiah Wedgwood. Instead, give them a precise enquiry question such as: Did Josiah Wedgwood play an important part in the anti-slavery movement? The Spartacus website at www.spartacus.schoolnet.co.uk/USAslavery.htm could be used for this enquiry.

The SHP website at www.tasc.ac.uk/shp lists website links relevant to the teaching of the SHP GCSE syllabus topics. A bulletin board style element is due to be added to the site which will allow teachers to exchange ideas and links.

Citizenship

This course can make a very useful contribution to citizenship education. It can help develop an understanding of the nature of community, roles and relationships in a democratic society, the nature of personal responsibility and rights in law and justice.

Literacy

Historical fiction plays an important part in people's perception of Britain's past. The study and use of historical fiction is part of this book. Reading and writing historical fiction allows pupils to see through the eyes of individuals in the past. It also allows teachers to gain a valuable insight into the level of understanding their pupils have of the period. This is one of the key conclusions of the EACH project (Teaching English and History using Historical Fiction), which has been running for seven years. It is this development that underpins the Story Writing activity on Children in the mills on page 23 of the Pupils' Book.

For more information on the EACH project visit www.dorset-lea.org.uk/projects/each where you can post examples of your pupils' completed stories.

Religious education

The most important religious change between 1750 and 1900 was the decline of the Church of England and the rise of nonconformity. The key theme, which occurs in several of the depth studies, is how religious belief affected people's actions such as the provision of education for the poor or the campaign to abolish slavery. These are explicitly examined as part of the final depth study on Victorian values.

DETAILED TEACHERS' NOTES

OVERVIEW

Timeline
- Pupils' Book pp. vi–1
- Support material: Worksheets 1, 2; SNSM TRB Task 1

Ideally, before you start this unit cover one wall of the classroom with a large timeline. As the class works through the unit, pupils can add the events they have studied and gradually form a class display.

Worksheet 1 provides a basic timeline for pupils' own notes. This can be used with Worksheet 2 which provides pictures for pupils to identify, label and place on the timeline to help develop their basic grasp of chronology.

You may support this activity by using the timeline (see SNSM TRB Task 1). Seeing how different parts of the period relate to each other is important for developing pupils' understanding.

How did Britain change between 1750 and 1900?
- Pupils' Book pp. 1–9
- Support material: Worksheets 3, 4; SNSM TRB Tasks 2, 3, 4; SNSM Picture Pack; SNSM Picture Pack Workbook Tasks 2, 3, 4

This introductory enquiry aims to provide pupils with a framework of the unit as a whole. The first spread contrasts the start and finish dates of the period. The two pictures are designed to signpost clearly the changes between 1750 and 1900. You can support this with SNSM Picture Pack Workbook Task 2.

The next three spreads give snapshots of 1750, 1825 and 1900 respectively, with the information grouped clearly into six categories:

- Population
- Work
- Education
- Health and medicine
- The vote
- Travel

These categories reflect the broad concerns of the unit as a whole. It is important to recognise from the beginning that these categories are not fixed. There are overlaps, for example between Population and Health and medicine. It is useful for pupils to discuss these possible links and overlaps.

The Activity on page 4 is intended to divide the categories amongst a whole class and to begin the task by asking pupils to make notes on their chosen category for each of the three dates. Worksheet 3 consists of a set of recording cards which are designed to support pupils' note making and also to enable them to manipulate the information physically, in order to identify links and overlaps. Worksheet 4 is designed to give additional support to those pupils allocated the Work and the Population categories. On page 9, Question 1 asks pupils to describe the changes they can find whilst Question 2 asks them to explain the changes. Finally, the Discuss questions on page 9 are intended to help pupils to gain an overview of the period and the changes within it. They also challenge pupils to make a distinction between change and progress.

You can also support this task with the Population and the Health and Medicine cards from SNSM TRB Task 2, and extend it with the Transport and the Work cards. Please note that these do require careful explanation for pupils.

Your pathway
- Pupils' Book p. 10

This page should act as a 'route planner' through the course. Make sure that the pupils are aware of what they are going to be studying, and discuss with them how each enquiry and activity will help them to gain a better understanding of the period. Fitting together the different components and examining where they overlap are crucial to developing pupils' understanding.

DEPTH STUDY 1: The Industrial Revolution

- Pupils' Book p. 11

Use the painting on page 11 as a stimulus for discussion. This is an opportunity to hook pupils' interest. Questions to pose might be: What industries are shown? Are the workmen strong and healthy? What new developments are hinted at, such as newspapers? What other objects/details are included and what is their significance? What is the purpose of putting the little girl in the picture?

The text on page 11 clearly focuses this depth study not so much on what happened during the Industrial Revolution but on how the Industrial Revolution affected the lives of people at different levels of society. This is the reason for looking at Wedgwood, Arkwright and the children working in the cotton mills. The major focus is on the cotton industry. The Review Activity on page 32 (How did the Industrial Revolution change things?) pulls all this together.

Why was British industry so successful?

- Pupils' Book pp. 12–13
- Support material: Worksheet 5

The key objective of this spread is for pupils to understand why the Industrial Revolution happened. The talking heads of contemporary characters are used to make concrete the multiplicity of factors. The Activity on page 12 is designed to ensure pupils have a lasting record which will support their work in the rest of this section. **Worksheet 5** provides a format for recording the information.

Case study 1: What made Josiah Wedgwood successful?

- Pupils' Book pp. 14–15

This case study invites pupils to think about the factors that led to the Industrial Revolution in the context of a successful individual, Josiah Wedgwood. The Discuss activity on page 14 asks pupils to consider which of the factors from pages 12–13 were relevant in his case. The third question goes up a level and asks them to explain how these factors helped him. Finally, for extension they have to decide which factor was the most important.

Implicit within Wedgwood's story are the changes in working practices he brought about, in particular the division of labour. Pupils should be asked to consider how these new practices affected the working lives of Wedgwood's potters.

Case study 2: What made Richard Arkwright successful?

- Pupils' Book pp. 16–21
- Support material: Worksheets 6, 7, 8; SNSM TRB Tasks 5, 6

The same two themes – what made him successful and what impact did the changes he made have on the lives of his workers – run through this section on Richard Arkwright.

Like Wedgwood, Arkwright was the youngest of 13. This is an opportunity to discuss coincidence and also family size in the period.

Pages 16–19

These two spreads tell the story of Arkwright and his business success, and highlight the development of the factory system which had a massive impact on the lives of ordinary people. The Discuss activity on page 17 focuses on Arkwright's steps to success. **Worksheet 7** is designed to help pupils with Question 4 in which they are asked to make a comparison between Wedgwood and Arkwright. The Activity on page 17 is designed to pull together all aspects of Arkwright's life and business career. **Worksheet 6** and **SNSM TRB Task 5** are intended to support pupils in preparing their story strip, which is the key written outcome. This activity is also intended to help focus pupils' use of pages 18–21.

The Discuss activity on page 19 is designed to help pupils to think about the environmental and heritage issues associated with Cromford Mill.

Pages 20–21

The sources and Discuss activity on page 21 explore the differing interpretations of Richard Arkwright over time and invite pupils to assess his significance as an individual. **SNSM TRB Task 6** supports this. **Worksheet 8** offers a different perspective on the role of the individual during the Industrial Revolution.

Scoring for Worksheet 8: we've given three points for what we consider to be the best idea in the context of nineteenth-century business, and one for the worst. These are not intended to be right and wrong answers, and you might disagree with our scoring. For question 4 we've scored two options as 'equal best'. Our suggestions are:

Q1: a=1, b=3, c=2   Q4: a=1, b=3, c=3
Q2: a=2, b=1, c=3   Q5: a=2, b=3, c=1
Q3: a=1, b=3, c=2   Q6: a=2, b=3, c=1

Children in the mills

- Pupils' Book pp. 22–29
- Support material: Worksheets 9, 10, 11; SNSM TRB Tasks 22, 23, 24; SNSM Picture Pack; SNSM Picture Pack Workbook Task 5

The purpose of these pages is to explore the myth and reality of working conditions for children in cotton mills. The historical fiction activity on page 23 is designed to give a clear purpose to pupils' research. The story recipe is most important; it gives creative constraints for pupils to work within. Without it pupils may try to be too ambitious, to have too many characters, settings and events. **Worksheet 9** gives positive and explicit guidance on how to write historical fiction and provides a planning sheet. The production of a complete story may be the outcome for some pupils. For others, part of a story, a character description or just a plan may be the significant outcome.

Worksheet 10 provides an annotated copy of Source 4 on page 25 which will give pupils some ideas for the Story Writing activity, help them with the setting and suggest possible jobs for the characters.

The testimony to the Parliamentary Select Committee (Sources 10–14 on pages 28–29) should provide a good source of plot ideas for pupils to exploit. There is a very clear link here with literacy. **SNSM TRB Task 22** and **SNSM Picture Pack Workbook Task 5** give good support here. It is important to make sure that pupils have feedback on their story writing from both you as teacher and also from their peers. This is an essential part of the creative process.

SNSM TRB Tasks 23 and 24 offer an additional or alternative perspective here.

As the conditions of children working in mills became such a controversial subject at the time, any source material relating to it provides an excellent opportunity for the consideration of source reliability and utility. This is highlighted by the SOURCE WARNING! device on pages 26–31. For each source stamped you could draw attention to what information can be taken from it and then go on to discuss author, audience and purpose. You can help pupils to see that just because a source is biased does not mean that it is not useful.

The Discuss activities on pages 27–28 are designed to help pupils consider the reliability of sources. **Worksheet 11** provides support for pupils by encouraging them to physically mark the record of interviews at the Parliamentary Commission.

Robert Owen: a better way to run a factory?
■ Pupils' Book pp. 30–31

The inclusion of Robert Owen is important for pupils to appreciate that not all mills were the same and to see the dangers of stereotyping in history.

Review: How did the Industrial Revolution change things?
■ Pupils' Book p. 32

This Review Activity is intended to pull the whole enquiry together. The use of a spider diagram is suggested, as the historical fiction story is the key written outcome of this section. The central organising idea has been how the Industrial Revolution affected people's lives. Pupils are now equipped with an understanding of how it changed

the lives of people at two levels of industrial society. Their discussion in pairs and completed diagrams should consolidate this understanding.

DEPTH STUDY 2: Empire and trade

Use the map on page 33 as a stimulus for discussion. This is an opportunity to hook pupils' interest. Questions to pose might be: Which islands and countries are shown in pink? What countries are these today? You could list these on the board and make a link to the Commonwealth if appropriate. Go on to invite questions from pupils which revolve around the issues of why the Empire was so big and how we acquired it. This then leads into the enquiry.

What was the British Empire for?
■ Pupils' Book pp. 34–35
■ Support material: SNSM TRB Tasks 40, 41

This introductory spread is intended to define clearly the British Empire, including its physical extent. It also highlights the key question, which is not so much whether it was a good or bad thing but rather what impact it had on the lives of people in different parts of the Empire, on the Imperialists and the Imperialised. **SNSM TRB Task 40** is intended to make this very concrete.

When pupils study Source 2 draw their attention to the words in the centre: THE EMPIRE ON WHICH THE SUN NEVER SETS.

Why does London need new docks?
■ Pupils' Book pp. 36–37
■ Support material: Worksheet 12

The straightforward Activity on page 37 is intended to show the impact of the British Empire on trade by focusing on the major port of London. The need for new docks is a clear indicator of the growth in trade. **Worksheet 12** is a writing frame to support those pupils who need a model for this form of writing.

Britain's slave trade: the inside story
■ Pupils' Book pp. 38–49
■ Support material: Worksheet 13; SNSM TRB Tasks 29, 30, 39; SNSM Picture Pack; SNSM Picture Pack Workbook Task 12

A useful starting point to the study of the West African slave trade would be to look at other examples pupils may have already encountered in

Ancient Greece and the Roman Empire. Many schools also look briefly at the West African kingdoms of Ghana and Mali which rivalled contemporary European states. Slavery had long been a part of the culture of the region. Slaves were seen as useful and helpful people, whose ownership carried with it specific obligations – to feed, to clothe, to shelter and protect. To the king and noblemen they were also a status symbol, and necessary to the maintenance of rank. This theme of the protection afforded by a great man to his slaves was part of town and village life, and formed a parallel to the serf system of feudal Europe. But the arrival of the European slave traders changed the nature and scale of slavery.

The driving force behind pupils' work on this enquiry is to prepare an anti-slavery campaign. This Activity is outlined on page 39. Pupils will need to gather material to support their case. A variety of forms of presentation are possible but it is important to ensure that pupils are not sidetracked by the demands of presentation at the expense of substance. It is the message not the medium that is key here. Support is available from **Worksheet 13**, which is a note-making frame. Pupils are prompted by Activity boxes at each stage as they work through the enquiry.

SNSM TRB Task 29 supports work on the slave ship *Zong*, **Task 30** provides an optional case study for pupils to use here, whilst **Task 39** offers a simplified treatment of the slave trade triangle.

SNSM Picture Pack Workbook Task 12 also gives a simplified treatment of the slave trade triangle as well as the life of slaves on plantations.

Why was slavery abolished?
■ Pupils' Book pp. 50–53
■ Support material: Worksheet 14; SNSM TRB Task 31

This section builds upon the pupils' own anti-slavery campaign. Central to it is an understanding that there are no simple explanations for historical events. This underpins the Activity on page 51. The quality of pupils' thinking is more important here than any written outcome. **Worksheet 14** provides a larger copy of the diagram for pupils to use. **SNSM TRB Task 31** provides an alternative route to the same historical conclusion.

Britain and India: joined by a thread
■ Pupils' Book pp. 54–59

This section makes explicit how the British exploited their Empire. The Indian cotton industry was deliberately destroyed to benefit the Lancashire cotton industry. This can provide a good link into the National Curriculum area of study, a world

study after 1900. When Gandhi visited Lancashire in 1931, British cotton workers asked him to call off the Indian cotton boycott which was putting them out of work. This reinforces how the two were inextricably linked. The Activity on page 59 should pull these threads together.

The Discuss activity on page 58 tackles the difficult problem of how the very words we use to describe the past colour the picture we give. A mutiny and a revolution are two very different things. Challenge pupils to decide which word we should have used in each part of the text on pages 58–59.

Review: Who benefited from the Empire?
■ Pupils' Book p. 60
■ Support material: Worksheet 15

The challenge of the Review Activity is for pupils to try to give a balanced view of the British Empire, of who benefited and, conversely, who did not. They need to be steered away from a simplistic answer that says that the Empire was a good or bad thing. The plate is reproduced on **Worksheet 15** with space for pupils to add their annotations.

DEPTH STUDY 3:
Towns

This depth study focuses on why people moved to towns and what it was like to live there.

Use the engraving on page 61 as a stimulus for discussion. This is an opportunity to hook pupils' interest. A question to focus pupils might be: What would be bad about living here? The sort of responses to expect are about overcrowding, unsanitary/unhealthy conditions, and noise and smoke pollution from railways.

Foul facts!
■ Pupils' Book pp. 62–65
■ Support material: Worksheets 16, 17; SNSM TRB Tasks 3, 4; SNSM Picture Pack; SNSM Picture Pack Workbook Task 6

The key question throughout this enquiry is: Why did people choose to live in towns if they were so horrible? The Activity on page 62 is the starting point. It exploits the populist approach of the 'Horrible Histories' series. The pupils' completed 'ten foul facts' will constitute a stereotypical view that they can go on to investigate and eventually challenge. Pupils should be encouraged to use all of this section, particularly pages 82–83, and not just to take their foul facts from pages 62–65.

Worksheet 16 gives pupils some ideas for the Activity on page 62, whilst **Worksheet 17** supports pupils in completing the Activity on page 65.

Were they pushed or were they pulled?
■ Pupils' Book pp. 66–67

This spread encourages pupils to consider the motivation of people who moved into the rapidly growing towns. It supports pupils in developing a rounded view of Victorian towns.

Why did Liverpool and Manchester need a railway?
■ Pupils' Book pp. 68–73
■ Support material: Worksheets 18, 19; SNSM TRB Tasks 17, 18, 19; SNSM Picture Pack; SNSM Picture Pack Workbook Tasks 9, 10

These spreads outline the need for the railway, the stages in planning and building, and the effect the completed railway had. The Discuss activity, which begins on page 69, invites pupils to see events through the eyes of four different individuals representing different interest groups. This then builds through the chronology of the railway with additional activities on pages 71 and 73.
Worksheets 18 and 19 both support this activity.

SNSM TRB Tasks 17, 18 and 19 provide an alternative route through this enquiry.

Beside the sea!
■ Pupils' Book pp. 74–77

These spreads pick up on the growth of towns in the period, offer a contrast to the 'foul' stereotype and make a connection with India. This connection is the presence of Sake Deen Mahomed and the design of the Prince Regent's palace, the Royal Pavilion. The Activity on page 75 concentrates on pupils recording change between 1825 and 1850 preparatory to their discussion and the more difficult questions on page 77. This change in one town reflects the changes in society as a whole. Any town in this period will reflect change, often due to the arrival of railways. Trade directories are a good source for examining this. These were printed from the mid-eighteenth century onwards by various publishers, Kelly being the most famous. The directories give information about the inhabitants of a town listing their names, addresses and occupations. They can be used to gain a picture of economic activity in a town over a period of time and can be found in most local reference libraries.

The different faces of London
■ Pupils' Book pp. 78–83
■ Support material: Worksheets 20, 21; SNSM TRB Tasks 11, 42

This section deliberately looks at different dimensions of the capital. London could show all five different faces depending upon which aspect you chose to look at or to emphasise. This should finally reinforce for pupils the need to consider all aspects of towns. The Activity on page 78 invites pupils to set up two contrasting interpretations.

The Activity on page 83 highlights the problems of living in the East End and is based upon actual evidence for Charles Booth's report. **Worksheets 20 and 21** help pupils complete Questions 1 and 2. Please note 2–3 copies of Worksheet 20 are needed per pupil. Additional support is available from **SNSM TRB Task 42**.

Review: Was there more to a Victorian town than 'foul facts'?
■ Pupils' Book p. 84
■ Support material: SNSM TRB Task 10

This review page returns to the key question: Why did people choose to live in towns if they were so horrible? The pupils' completed 'ten foul facts' constitute a stereotypical view that they can go on to challenge with their 'Beyond the foul facts…' This could provide a springboard for discussion of populist interpretations of history in books such as the 'Horrible Histories' series or on television and film.

DEPTH STUDY 4:
The vote

What was wrong with democracy in the 1820s?
■ Pupils' Book pp. 86–91
■ Support material: Worksheets 22, 23; SNSM TRB Task 37

This section makes a clear contribution to Citizenship. Particularly relevant is the Activity on page 87 comparing the system in 1820 to today. **Worksheet 22** is designed to help with this. The first two spreads are intended to make clear what was wrong in the eyes of people at the time. **SNSM TRB Task 37** backs this up. The working class radical introduced on page 89 acts as a commentator on the changes that follow.

The Activity on page 91 gives pupils the opportunity to summarise the arguments. Their ability to draw is not crucial here. Whilst it will give an opportunity for some pupils to shine, it is perfectly possible to sketch out an outline using words. The best support for pupils is to examine closely Sources 1 and 2, other modern political cartoons and **Worksheet 23**.

Were the Chartists revolutionaries?

■ Pupils' Book pp. 92–97
■ Support material: Worksheets 24, 25; SNSM TRB Task 38

The overall direction of this enquiry is to consider whether or not the Chartists were revolutionaries. Associated themes here are the diversity of the movement in terms of its supporters, objectives and methods, and the response of the government. The postscript on page 97 is important to signal that whilst the Chartists did not achieve their Charter demands, they were not failures. They ran a successful mass movement complete with its own newspaper and they influenced many people. Individual Chartists continued to work for causes that helped the working classes such as teetotalism.

Activities **A** and **B** on pages 92–93 ask pupils to decide whether the Chartist aims were revolutionary.

Pages 94–95 use the Newport Rising as an example of Chartist violence for pupils to consider. **Worksheet 24** provides a version of Source 6 on page 95 for pupils to mark. This is also an ideal opportunity to contrast two interpretations of the same event. The main theme is then continued and the final Activity on page 97 pulls the whole together. **Worksheet 25** provides guidance on how to write the radio programme for Activity B on page 97 and includes a blank radio planning sheet. An alternative route through Chartism is provided by **SNSM TRB Task 38**.

Review: Did anything really change?

■ Pupils' Book p. 98

This page seeks to draw the section to a clear conclusion. The speech bubble activity in Question 1 serves as a preparation for pupils to write their final answer in Question 2.

DEPTH STUDY 5:
Victorian values

Use the painting and questions on page 99 as a stimulus for discussion. This is an opportunity to hook pupils' interest. Explicit support is provided by **Worksheet 26**.

What did the Victorians believe?

■ Pupils' Book pp. 100–105
■ Support material: Worksheet 27; SNSM Picture Pack; SNSM Picture Pack Workbook Tasks 18, 20

The speech bubbles and value cards are intended to give a change of pace, allowing pupils to concentrate on one source at a time whilst building towards an overview picture of what the Victorians believed. **Worksheet 27** provides a set of value cards for pupils to use. The value cards are used later in the final Review Activity on page 112. The device of Mr Oaks is intended to make this depth study easier by personalising the abstract ideas.

How did the Victorians try to help the poor?

■ Pupils' Book pp. 106–109
■ Support material: SNSM TRB Tasks 33, 34, 35, 36; SNSM Picture Pack; SNSM Picture Pack Workbook Task 19

As charity was such an important idea to the Victorians it is treated separately. But the device of the value cards continues. The focus is on the Poor Law – a link is possible back to Chartism here – and the workhouse system. The activities on page 107 invite pupils to consider the ideas behind the Victorians' actions and to look at our ideas today. **SNSM TRB Tasks 33, 34 and 35** offer support here.

The story of Harriet Kettle on pages 108–109 shows the system operating in the case of one individual. **SNSM TRB Task 36** is an alternative route to exploring her life.

Why did Annie Besant want to help poor people?

■ Pupils' Book pp. 110–111
■ Support material: SNSM TRB Task 28; SNSM Picture Pack; SNSM Picture Pack Workbook Task 14

The case of Annie Besant is a chance to focus on the ideas of yet another individual within the Victorian period. This spread also allows for some source evaluation work and picks up again on the links with India. **SNSM TRB Task 28** is an alternative route to exploring her life.

Review: Victorian values

■ Pupils' Book p. 112

This final Review Activity enables pupils to think about the second half of this period of study – that which is labelled Victorian. It invites them to reach a judgement and asks them to support it with evidence. Ideally, pupils will recognise how difficult it is to characterise a whole period.

Timeline: Britain 1750–1900

1900

1875

1850

1825

1800

1775

1750

Re-Discovering Britain 1750–1900 Teachers' Resource Book © John Murray

Where does it fit?

The six pictures below show different people or events from the period 1750–1900.

1 Cut out each picture and place it in the correct position on the timeline on Worksheet 1.

2 Write a caption for the picture.

3 When you study that person or event, write a sentence explaining why it is important enough to be selected as one of the six people or events for the timeline.

4 Suggest six other people or events that you would put on this timeline.

How did Britain change between 1750 and 1900?

Use these cards to help you with the Activities on pages 4 and 9.

Population – 1750

In 1750 _____

_____

_____

Work – 1750

In 1750 _____

_____

_____

Population – 1825

In 1825 _____

_____

_____

The changes since 1750 _____

_____

_____

_____

Work – 1825

In 1825 _____

_____

_____

The changes since 1750 _____

_____

_____

_____

Population – 1900

In 1900 _____

_____

_____

The changes since 1825 _____

_____

_____

_____

Work – 1900

In 1900 _____

_____

_____

The changes since 1825 _____

_____

_____

_____

Use these cards to help you with the Activities on pages 4 and 9.

Education – 1750

In 1750 _____

_____

_____

Health and medicine – 1750

In 1750 _____

_____

_____

Education – 1825

In 1825 _____

_____

_____

The changes since 1750 _____

_____

_____

_____

Health and medicine – 1825

In 1825 _____

_____

_____

The changes since 1750 _____

_____

_____

_____

Education – 1900

In 1900 _____

_____

_____

The changes since 1825 _____

_____

_____

_____

Health and medicine – 1900

In 1900 _____

_____

_____

The changes since 1825 _____

_____

_____

_____

Use these cards to help you with the Activities on pages 4 and 9.

The vote – 1750

In 1750 _____
_____
_____

Travel – 1750

In 1750 _____
_____
_____

The vote – 1825

In 1825 _____
_____
_____

The changes since 1750 _____
_____
_____
_____

Travel – 1825

In 1825 _____
_____
_____

The changes since 1750 _____
_____
_____
_____

The vote – 1900

In 1900 _____
_____
_____

The changes since 1825 _____
_____
_____
_____

Travel – 1900

In 1900 _____
_____
_____

The changes since 1825 _____
_____
_____
_____

Major cities and industries

1 Use this worksheet to help you with the Activity on page 4.
2 Compare the three maps and make a note underneath of the changes that occurred.
3 Write a sentence to describe how the population has changed.

_____

_____

_____

_____

4 Write another sentence to describe what changes have happened to industry.

_____

_____

_____

_____

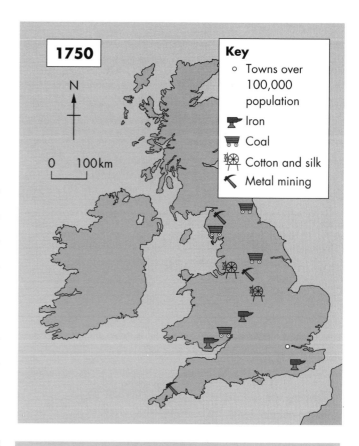

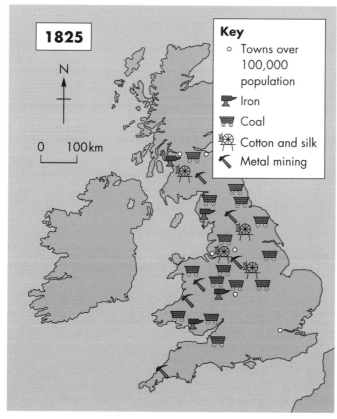

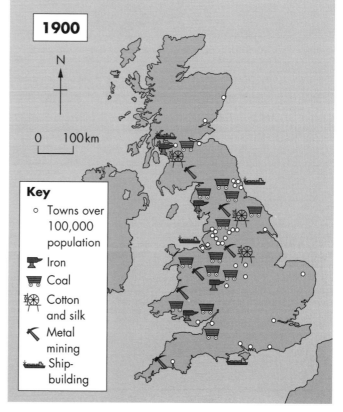

_____   _____

_____   _____

_____   _____

Why was British industry so successful?

Use this worksheet to help you make notes for the Activity on page 12.
Keep your answers safe. You will need them later.

More food

_____
_____
_____
_____
_____
_____

Growing overseas trade

_____
_____
_____
_____
_____
_____

Plenty of raw materials

_____
_____
_____
_____
_____
_____

Better transport

_____
_____
_____
_____
_____
_____

Growing population

_____
_____
_____
_____
_____
_____

Talented individuals

_____
_____
_____
_____
_____
_____

What made Richard Arkwright successful?

Use this worksheet to make your story strip for the Activity on page 17. You can either draw pictures in the boxes or describe what the pictures should show.

1 As a child Arkwright worked for a barber, but he was very ambitious and wanted to start his own business …

2

3

4

5

6

7

8

9

10

Wedgwood or Arkwright?

Use this worksheet to help you develop your answer to Question 4 of the Discuss activity on page 17.

Wedgwood and Arkwright were both important businessmen. But was one more important than the other? Has one had more lasting influence on people's lives to this day? Use the following table to organise your thoughts about the importance of these two businessmen.

	Wedgwood	Arkwright
What did he invent?		
How successful a businessman was he?		
How did he treat his workers?		
How much influence have the changes he made had on other people's lives since his lifetime?		

Would you have made a good businessman or woman?

You have read about two successful businessmen, Wedgwood and Arkwright. Would you have made a successful businessman or woman?

Look at the following problems that businessmen faced during this period. Decide which course of action you would have taken in each case. You must give a reason for your choice.

Your teacher will then help you add up your score and you will see how well you would have succeeded as a businessman or woman.

Your score
15–18: You are a brilliant entrepreneur.
10–15: You make some good decisions, but you are a bit too cautious.
6–9: You've got a lot to learn about business!

---

1 Your business has at last made a profit. Do you:
  a) spend the money on a new house for your family *or* ☐
  b) invest the money in the business to buy the latest machinery *or* ☐
  c) leave the money in the bank to earn interest? ☐

2 You have just invented a new spinning machine. Do you:

  a) keep the invention a secret *or* ☐
  b) boast to everyone about your invention and let them borrow it *or* ☐
  c) take out a patent on the invention? ☐

3 You own a textile factory. You need more workers. Do you:
  a) employ the cheapest workers you can find, and save money by paying them very little and spending nothing on their welfare *or* ☐
  b) employ the fittest and strongest workers you can find, then work them as hard as you can until they drop from exhaustion *or* ☐
  c) employ the fittest workers you can find and look after them: educate their children; build decent housing for them? ☐

4 You own a pottery business. You sell all your products locally. Do you:

  a) carry on as you are *or* ☐
  b) advertise your products all over the country *or* ☐
  c) carry out research to see what new products are needed to widen your markets? ☐

5 You run an iron works. You are being charged more and more for your raw materials – coal, iron ore and limestone – by the local mine and quarry owners. Do you:

  a) try to find a new source of raw materials from further afield *or* ☐
  b) buy up the local mines and quarries *or* ☐
  c) charge your customers more for your iron? ☐

6 There's a great demand for bricks to build houses in the growing new towns. You run a successful brick works. Do you:

  a) save up the profits until you have enough money in a few years' time to extend your brick works *or* ☐
  b) bring in a partner with money to extend your brick works now *or* ☐
  c) sell off your business to a rival while things are going well? ☐

Trouble at the mill

Use this worksheet to help you with the Story Writing activity on page 23.

Before you begin to write make sure you have decided whether your story is going to be told in the first person by one of your characters, or by an unseen narrator using the third person.

Look at your story planning table and the notes you have made to help you.

Setting
- Don't forget to use the illustrations in your book to help you create descriptions of setting, particularly the mill on page 25. You can refer to artefacts used in mills to help to create a sense of place in your story.
- Remember to use alliteration sometimes when describing places.
- Adjectives are an excellent way of creating strong descriptions of places, but be careful – don't overuse them or write long list sentences as these are boring.

Characters
- Some possible characters are a mill owner, an overseer, child and adult workers.
- You can develop rounded characters by describing what they say and what they do as well as by describing their physical appearance.
- Use descriptive verbs and adverbs when you write about characters.
- Similes can be an excellent way of suggesting what a character is like.

Plot
- What event or situation starts the story off and provides the reason for what the characters do?
- Stories usually have a problem which the characters must solve. There are some possible story problems suggested in this section. Could you use one of these to help you plan your story?
- Is the problem about something that is lost such as a child's lunch?
- Could the problem be caused by something someone does? Is there a small child being unfairly punished by an adult?
- Is the problem a language confusion between some of David Dale's Gaelic-speaking workers and an English-speaking foreman?
- Is the problem a result of the characters' reactions to an accident or event such as a visit by the mill owner?

When you have decided on your setting, characters and plot, think about how you will write your opening paragraph.

Conflicts
- What important things happen as a result of the initial problem?
- Are the things that happen believable and do they match your factory setting?
- How do your characters cope with the conflicts?

Endings
- Has the problem been sorted out?
- Has everything important been explained?
- Think about your final paragraph: what sort of ending have you chosen? Will you leave things open for a sequel, provide a shock or move the reader gently away from your characters, like the closing shots of a film?

Story planner

Use this story planner to help you to plan your story.

Setting:

_____
_____
_____
_____
_____

Characters:

_____   _____   _____
_____   _____   _____
_____   _____   _____
_____   _____   _____

Plot:

_____
_____
_____
_____
_____
_____

Conflicts: **Endings:**

_____   _____
_____   _____
_____   _____
_____   _____
_____   _____
_____   _____

Activities at the mill

Use this worksheet to help you with the Story Writing activity on page 25.

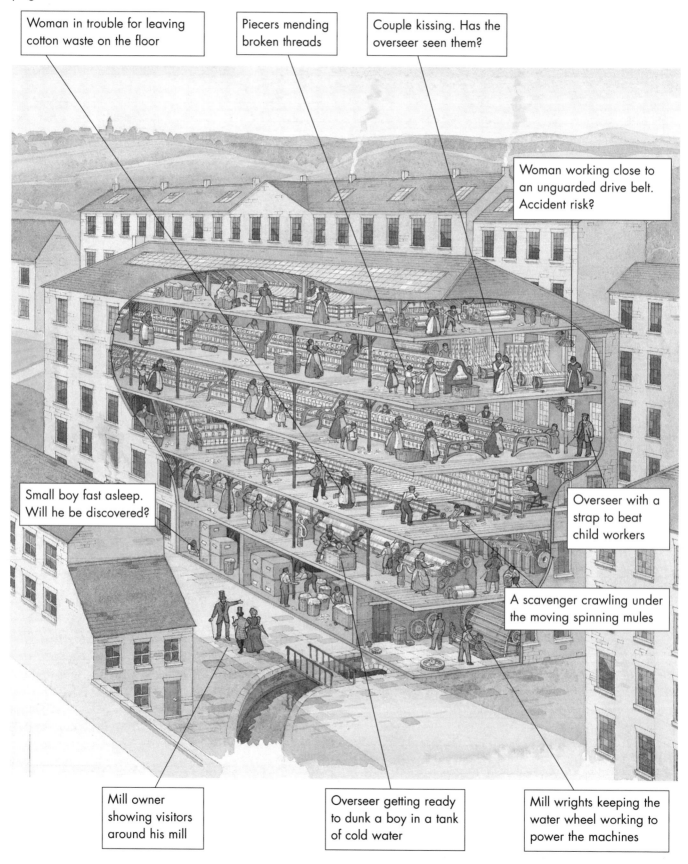

Woman in trouble for leaving cotton waste on the floor

Piecers mending broken threads

Couple kissing. Has the overseer seen them?

Woman working close to an unguarded drive belt. Accident risk?

Small boy fast asleep. Will he be discovered?

Overseer with a strap to beat child workers

A scavenger crawling under the moving spinning mules

Mill owner showing visitors around his mill

Overseer getting ready to dunk a boy in a tank of cold water

Mill wrights keeping the water wheel working to power the machines

Re-Discovering Britain 1750–1900 Teachers' Resource Book © John Murray

Were witnesses at the Parliamentary Select Committee in 1831 asked leading questions?

Use this worksheet to help you with the Discuss activity on page 28.

A leading question is one that contains suggestions about how the interviewee should answer.

Read Sources 13 and 14 below.

Highlight on this worksheet any questions that you think are leading.

▼ SOURCE 13 *Eliza Marshall*

Q. What were your hours of work?

A. When I first went to the mill we worked from six in the morning till seven in the evening. After a time we began at five in the morning, and worked till ten at night.

Q. Were you very much fatigued by that length of labour?

A. Yes.

Q. Did they beat you?

A. When I was younger they used to do it often.

Q. Did the labour affect your limbs?

A. Yes, when we worked over-hours I was worse by a great deal; I had stuff to rub my knees; and I used to rub my joints a quarter of an hour, and sometimes an hour or two.

Q. Were you straight before that?

A. Yes, I was; my master knows that well enough; and when I have asked for my wages, he said that I could not run about as I had been used to.

Q. Are you crooked now?

A. Yes, I have an iron on my leg; my knee is contracted.

Q. Have the surgeons in the Infirmary told you by what your deformity was occasioned [caused]?

A. Yes, one of them said it was by standing; the marrow is dried out of the bone, so that there is no natural strength in it.

Q. You were quite straight till you had to labour so long in those mills?

A. Yes, I was as straight as any one.

▼ SOURCE 14 *John Hall, overseer*

Q. Do you live at Bradford?

A. Yes.

Q. Are you the overseer of Mr John Wood?

A. I am.

Q. Will you have the goodness to state the present hours of working in your factory?

A. Our present hours are from six till seven.

Q. With what intervals for rest and refreshment?

A. Half an hour for breakfast and forty minutes for dinner.

Q. Do you believe that children can endure the labour you have been describing without injury?

A. No, I do not.

Q. When your hands [children] have been employed for some time do you see any alteration in their appearance?

A. In the course of a few weeks I see a paleness in their faces, and they grow spiritless and tired.

Q. Have you remarked [noticed that] the cases of deformity are very common in Bradford?

A. They are very common. I have the names of, I think, about two hundred families I have visited myself that have deformed children, and I have taken particular care not to put down one single case where it might have happened by accident, but only those whom I judge to have been thrown crooked by the practice of piecing.

Why does London need new docks?

Use this writing frame to help you with the Activity on page 37.

Armstrong House
London

4th January 1800

To The Right Honourable William Pitt

Dear Sir

I am writing to you on behalf of the merchants of London to ask for your support.
We wish to build new docks for a number of reasons.

Firstly, there is Britain's world trade which _____

_____

_____

_____

_____

Secondly, there is the coastal trade which _____

_____

_____

_____

_____

The existing docks just cannot cope. Amongst the problems we currently face
there is _____

_____

_____

_____

_____

As merchants we are prepared to invest our own money in the construction of these
docks. We plan to use the docks ourselves and to charge others to use them. In
order to do this we need the government's permission. Will you help us?

I remain your humble and obedient servant,

Britain's slave trade: the inside story

Use this sheet to help you with the note-making Activities on pages 39–49, in preparation for the campaign Activity on page 49. Copy the questions into your notebook and complete the answers. The first one has been started for you.

NOTE 1:
How did the slave trade start?

a) the role of African kings
African kings captured slaves and held them ready for sale on the coast.

b) the role of plantations owners
Plantation owners used slave labour to produce their crops, such as cotton, which was imported from the West Indies to Britain.

c) the role of British slave traders
_____
_____

d) _____
_____

NOTE 2:
Why was the slave trade so profitable?

a) demand for slaves _____

b) the trade triangle _____

NOTE 3:
How did British people benefit from the slave trade?

a) British businessmen or traders? _____

b) Ordinary Britons? _____

NOTE 4:
Examples of cruelty: how were slaves treated on the slave ships?

a) _____

b) _____

NOTE 5:
How were the slaves treated in the West Indies? Examples:

a) a slave sale _____

b) working conditions _____

c) punishments _____

d) health and disease _____

Why was slavery abolished?

Use this worksheet for the Activity on page 51.

1 In each circle of the diagram put your explanation of how this factor helped to abolish slavery. Give examples or evidence to support this explanation.

2 On the arrows write your explanation of how one factor linked to or helped the others.

3 Write a paragraph underneath the diagram to explain what it shows.

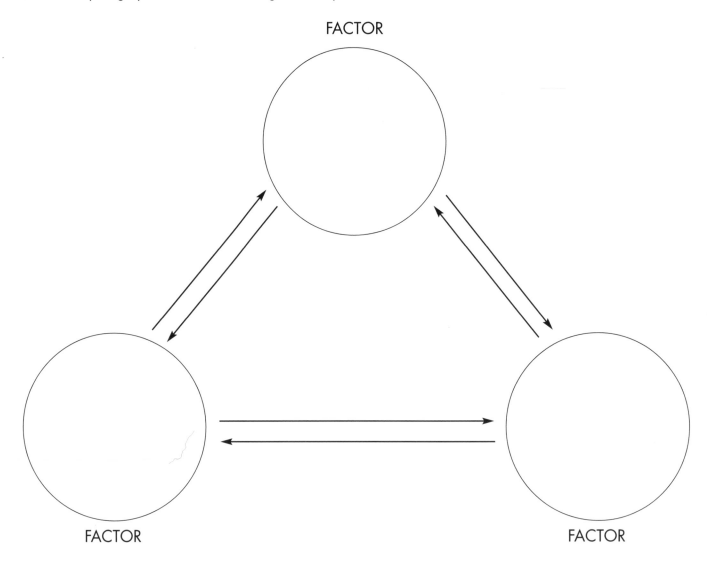

FACTOR

FACTOR

FACTOR

There are different reasons why slavery was abolished. This diagram

shows that _____

_____

_____

_____

_____

_____

_____

Re-Discovering Britain 1750–1900 Teachers' Resource Book   © John Murray

Who benefited from the Empire?

Use this worksheet for the Review Activity on page 60.

Foul facts 1

Use this worksheet to help you to compile your ten foul facts about towns
for the Activity on page 62.

▶ **SOURCE 1** *An extract from the Second Report into the Health of Towns 1845 that is describing the River Irwell and streams flowing through Manchester*

For many miles in its course it emits offensive smells, and bubbles of light carburetted hydrogen gas which rise to the surface. In all the streams an abundance of dead dogs and cats are to be seen in various stages of decomposition.

▶ **SOURCE 2** *Extracts from the Health of Towns Commission in 1843 describing Kidderminster*

The square Bewdley Road open privies, heaps of filth, muck holes full, well of water between two muck holes.

Unhealthy state of the courts and alleys in this Borough and nuisances arising from privies, slaughter houses and pig styes.

▶ **SOURCE 3** *Extract from Kellow Chesney's* The Victorian Underworld *published in 1970 in which he reconstructs Victorian London*

London's anomalies are endless. Among the packed buildings of the wealthiest city on earth rises the charnel-stench of grotesquely over brimming graveyards, protected by an alliance of parish interests and opponents of government interference. Besides the owners of slaughter-houses there are fat-boilers, glue-renderers, fell-mongers, tripe-scrapers, dig-skinners and the like, carrying on business whose fumes are recognised to be a gross public danger. Food and drink made from putrid and diseased ingredients, or adulterated with notoriously toxic substances are freely sold. In the face of constant public protest over the crowds of beggars and the burden of the poor, manufacturers continue to destroy their workpeople with phosphorous, lead, arsenic and other poisons.

▶ **SOURCE 4** *An engraving by Gustave Doré*

Foul facts 2

Use this worksheet to help you with the Activity on page 65.

Planning the Liverpool and Manchester Railway

Work in pairs. You are both industrialists who have to move goods
between Liverpool and Manchester. You have been asked to take part
in a survey to assess the region's transport needs. Fill it in using the
information on pages 68 and 69. Here are some suggestions:

- One of you could be transporting coal from Liverpool to Manchester.
- The other could be transporting cotton cloth from Manchester to
  Liverpool
- Invent a different role if you wish, but make sure it fits the facts on
  pages 68 and 69.

Committee of
Liverpool and Manchester
Industrialists

Name: _____

Please give some details of your business, e.g. what type of goods you have to move:

_____

_____

_____

Which route do you use at present?

_____

_____

Why do you use this route?

_____

_____

_____

Please give details of any problems you encounter in transporting your goods this way:

_____

_____

_____

_____

_____

_____

_____

Was the Liverpool and Manchester Railway a success?

1 Read sources 1 and 2, then think about how each of the people shown below could benefit from the Liverpool and Manchester Railway or be harmed by it.

2 Fill in their speech bubbles to show how each one might feel about the railway.

What people hoped would happen

▼ **SOURCE 1** *From the* Quarterly Review, *1825*

By the establishment of a railway, the inhabitants of Liverpool will be entitled to buy their coals several shillings per ton cheaper. By opening the collieries to the sea, Liverpool will become one of the greatest shipping ports for coal. A railway will help the conveyance of agricultural produce, and iron and limestone throughout the manufacturing districts of Lancashire. Nor are the advantages merely local. The journey from Manchester to Dublin will be reduced to eighteen or twenty hours, and the price of Irish corn, flax, linen and butter in Lancashire will be considerably reduced.

What did happen

▼ **SOURCE 2** *From the annual register in 1832, two years after the railway opened*

All the coaches have stopped running. The canals have reduced their prices by 30 per cent. Goods are delivered in Manchester the same day as they arrive in Liverpool. By canal it took three days. The saving to manufacturers in Manchester, in the transporting of cotton alone, has been £20,000 a year. Coal pits have been sunk and factories established along the railway, giving greater employment to the poor. The railway pays one fifth of the poor rates in the parishes through which it passes. The transportation of milk and garden produce is easier. Residents along the line can use the railways to attend their business in Manchester and Liverpool with ease and little expense. No inconvenience is felt by residents from smoke or noise. The value of land on the line has gone up because of the railway. It is much sought after for building.

A road owner

A Liverpool dock owner

A canal owner

A Manchester factory owner

Census form: Shelton Street

Use this worksheet to complete Question 1 on page 83.

Address and floor	Name	Gender	Age	Married/Single	Occupation													

Death report form: Shelton Street

Use this worksheet to complete Question 2 on page 83.

Address and floor	Name	Gender	Age at death	Cause of death

Democracy today

Use this worksheet to help you with the Activity on page 87.

	1820	**Today**
Constituencies		All of a roughly equal size so that everyone's vote is worth the same.
Who can vote?		Anyone over the age of 18 except for people certified as insane, lords and some criminals.
Who can be an MP?		Anyone over the age of 18. MPs are paid a salary.
Parties		Three main ones: Labour, Conservative and Liberal Democrat.
How does voting take place?		In secret. The candidate with most votes is elected as an MP.
When is there an election?		Every five years.
What do MPs do?	■ ■ ■	■ MPs join the House of Commons where they make decisions about how the country should be run. ■ The House of Commons is more important than the House of Lords. ■ The Prime Minister always comes from the House of Commons.

Cartoon ideas

Use this worksheet to help you with the Activity on page 91.

Ideas for a cartoon for reform

Ideas for a cartoon against reform

Other useful symbols could be used, for example the lion or dog for loyalty, or a rock for religion or the law. You can use words where necessary to make your meaning clearer.

You could also include symbols of the French Revolution to attack reformers, for example:

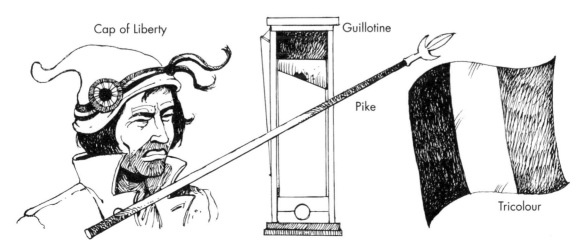

Cap of Liberty Guillotine Pike Tricolour

What happened at Newport on 4 November 1839?

Use this worksheet to help you with the Discussion questions on page 95.

Compare the two contemporary engravings of events at Newport in Source 6A and 6B.

1 Label each one to explain what it shows.
2 Underline in one colour any labels that show similarities between the pictures.
3 In another colour underline any labels that show differences.
4 Under each picture write a sentence explaining what impression it gives of the Chartists. Were they violent revolutionaries or orderly protesters?

Does this help you to decide who was to blame for the violence? Does it help you to decide if the methods used here by the Chartists were revolutionary?

▼ **SOURCE 6A**

_____

_____

Use this worksheet to help you with the Discussion questions on page 95.

▼ **SOURCE 6B**

_____

_____

_____

_____

Were the Chartists revolutionaries?

Use this planning sheet to help you with Activity B on page 97.

Radio programmes have to be carefully planned to run to time. They also have to be produced for a target audience. Your six-minute programme is to go out on a popular music radio station so it will have to be lively and snappy. One way to give your programme interest is to have different voices such as a Chartist or an historian speaking, not just the narrator. You may also want to include sound effects such as the noise of the crowd and shots fired at Newport in 1839. Some ideas are given in the sample planning sheet below.

As well as answering the key question, your programme should answer the following sub-questions:

1 What were the Chartists' aims?
2 What were the Chartists' methods?
3 How did the government react?
4 What did the Chartists achieve?

Programme narrator	**Programme notes and running time**	**Chartist**
Introduction		What we wanted was …
Revolutionaries or peaceful protestors: which of these were the Chartists?	Noise of shouting and cheering of a large crowd fades 5 seconds	
The Chartists were …		**Government minister**
The Chartists had a number of demands. Over to Chartist …	Introduction by narrator 20 seconds	The Newport rising confirmed our worst fears. It was revolution.
The Chartists campaigned in a number of different ways …	Chartist speaking demands 35 seconds	
		Historian A
	Narrator – how they campaigned 65 seconds	At Newport, despite the large numbers involved, there were hardly any reports of looting, vandalism or random violence. This shows that the Chartists were …
	Sound effect of Newport Rising 5 seconds	
		Historian B
	Government minister accusing Chartists of revolution 15 seconds …	…
		Sound effects
		Noise of a large crowd and shouting.
		Noise of a crowd, shouting in anger, smashing windows and shots being fired.

Programme narrator	Programme notes and running time	
		Chartist
		Government minister
		Historian A
		Historian B
		Sound effects
	Total: 6 minutes	

Work

▼ **SOURCE 1** *Extracts from Ford Madox Brown's own comments on his painting Work, 1863*

This picture was begun in 1852 at Hampstead. At that time extensive excavations, connected with the supply of water, were going on in the neighbourhood, and seeing and studying daily as I did the British navvy in the full swing of his activity, it appeared to me that he was at least as worthy of the powers of an English painter as the peasant of Campagna [in Italy]. Gradually this idea developed itself into that of *Work* as it now exists, with the British navvy for the central group as the outward and visible type of 'Work'.

- Here are represented the young navvy in the pride of manly health and beauty; the strong fully developed navvy who does his work and loves his beer; the selfish old stout bachelor navvy; the navvy of strong animal nature; and Paddy with his pipe in his mouth.

   The young navvy who occupies the place of hero in the picture stands on a platform placed half-way down the trench; two men from beneath shovel the earth up to him, and he shovels it on to the pile outside.
- Next in significance is the ragged wretch who has never been taught to work, with his restless gleaming eyes. He lives in Flower and Dean Street, where the policemen walk two and two. Before dawn you may see him miles out in the country, collecting his wild weeds and plants.
- In the opposite corner of the picture are two men who appear to have nothing to do. These are the brainworkers, who are seemingly idle.
- Next to these, on the shaded bank, are different characters out of work: haymakers in quest of employment; an Irishman with hay stuffed in his hat to keep the draught out; a young shoeless Irishman, with his wife, feeding their first-born with cold pap; an old sailor turned haymaker; and two young peasants in search of harvest work reduced in strength by lack of food.
- Behind the ragged wretch, appears a very different group who, from an opposite cause, have perhaps not been sufficiently used to work either. These are the rich, who have no need to work. The pastry-cook's tray, symbol of superfluity, accompanies these. Past the pastry-cook come two married ladies. The elder of the two has just flung a tract

entitled The Hodman's Haven or drink for thirsty souls to one of the navvies, who scorns it. This well-intentioned lady has perhaps never reflected that navvies may have notions to the effect that ladies might be benefited by receiving tracts containing navvies' ideas – as navvies are skilled workmen and men of great experience.

- In front of her is the lady whose only business in life as yet is to dress and look beautiful for our benefit. She probably possesses everything that can give enjoyment in life. Would anyone wish it otherwise? Certainly not I, dear lady. Only in your own interest, seeing that certain blessings like health and beauty cannot be insured for ever, I would beg to call your attention to the small, exceedingly ragged, dirty children in the foreground.
- They are motherless. As to the father, I have no doubt he drinks and neglects them. The eldest girl, not more than ten, is very worn looking and thin, her frock the gift of some grown-up person. However, the younger ones are taken care of, and nestle to her as to a mother. The sunburnt baby looks well fed and has even been put into mourning for mother. The other little one, though it sucks a carrot in place of a sugar-plum, and is shoeless, seems healthy and happy. The care of the two little ones is an anxious charge for the elder girl, and she has become a premature scold through having to manage that boy who is the plague of her life, as boys always are.
- The couple on horseback in the middle distance consists of a rich gentleman and his daughter. There is also a man with a beer tray. On the wall are posters; one of the Boy's Home, 41 Euston Road, which the lady giving out tracts will no doubt place the urchin playing with the barrow in. Back in the distance we see an Assembly Room where Professor Snoox is about to repeat his interesting lecture on the habits of the domestic cat. Indignant pusses up on the roofs are denying his theory in toto.
- In the background a policeman has caught an orange-girl in the heinous offence of resting her basket on a post, and who himself administers justice in the shape of a push, that sends her fruit all over the road.

1 Look again at your answers to the questions on page 99. Now that you have read the artist's notes on his own painting, how would you change your answers?

What did the Victorians believe?

Use this worksheet to help you with the Activity on page 100.

VALUE: Hard work and self-help
The Victorians believed that ...

VALUE: Modesty and decency
The Victorians believed that ...

VALUE: Family life
The Victorians believed that ...

VALUE: Charity
The Victorians believed that ...

VALUE: Obedience and respect
The Victorians believed that ...

VALUE: Religion
The Victorians believed that ...

VALUE: Knowing your place in society
The Victorians believed that ...

VALUE: Technology
The Victorians believed that ...

VALUE: Different roles for men and women
The Victorians believed that ...

VALUE: The British Empire
The Victorians believed that ...

RE-DISCOVERING
Britain
1750–1900

Re-Discovering Britain 1750–1900 is a fully revised, foundation edition of SHP's Britain 1750–1900 unit which was previously published as part of *Peace and War. Peace and War* was described by the TES as 'history teaching at its best'. This separate publication of Britain 1750–1900 keeps all the best features of that first edition while restructuring, redesigning and streamlining the unit, in the light of classroom use over the past few years, to make it more accessible.

This **Teachers' Resource Book** provides:
- detailed advice on teaching strategies and step-by-step guidance on how to use the activities in the Pupils' Book
- carefully selected photocopiable worksheets to support the activities in the Pupils' Book.

Further support for teaching Britain 1750–1900
In addition to this Teachers' Resource Book, the previously published *Special Needs Support Materials* Teachers' Resource Book and Picture Pack provide further opportunities for differentiation for pupils of all abilities.

	Teachers' Resource Book	Picture Pack	Picture Pack Workbook
Britain 1750–1900 SNSM	0 7195 7045 X	0 7195 7046 8	single copy: 0 7195 7227 4
			five pack: 0 7195 7234 7

The Re-Discovering Series	**Pupils' Book**	**Teachers' Resource Book**
Re-Discovering Medieval Realms	0 7195 8542 2	0 7195 8543 0
Re-Discovering the Making of the UK	0 7195 8544 9	0 7195 8545 7
Re-Discovering Britain 1750–1900	0 7195 8546 5	0 7195 8547 3
Re-Discovering the Twentieth Century World	0 7195 8548 1	0 7195 8549 X

ISBN 0-7195-8547-3

9 780719 585470 >

JOHN MURRAY